Coastal Carolina Sights

All these pictures & many more available for purchase at

www.marcwatkinsphotography.com

www.ingramcontent.com/pod-product-compliance
Lightning Source LLC
Chambersburg PA
CBHW060824290526
45792CB00005BB/1787